www.finishinglinepress.com

bastard bee

poems by

Jawn Van Jacobs

Finishing Line Press
Georgetown, Kentucky

bastard bee

ACKNOWLEDGMENTS

I would like to extend my heartfelt gratitude to the following journals for first publishing these poems and for their commitment to elevating queer voices:

bastard bee—Originally published in Issue 3 of *Moonday Magazine*
the beegeoisie—Originally published in *Bridge: Bluffton University's Literary Journal*
out of season—Originally published in *Beyond Queer Words*

Thank you for providing spaces where stories like mine can thrive and for fostering a community that celebrates authenticity and diversity. Your support means the world to me.

Publisher: Leah Huete de Maines
Editor: Christen Kincaid
Cover Art: Jawn Van Jacobs
Author Photo: Jawn Van Jacobs
Cover Design: Elizabeth Maines McCleavy

Order online: www.finishinglinepress.com
also available on amazon.com

Author inquiries and mail orders:
Finishing Line Press
PO Box 1626
Georgetown, Kentucky 40324
USA

Contents

for Remmy and Ethan—
may you always blow in the breezes
of bees & butterflies

bastard bee

i looked into a rose
& found a bastard bee—
drunken on the attar
of his daint residency

while others prided in clover
he licked from his Bourbons
an illegitimate strain of nectar
spurned by the populous

who sip at the same stamens
of society gone too often wrung—
emptied of dew by dawn
& withered by another's sun

March's duel

flowers gain their aegis
when winter will not abate—
the temperatures on horseback joust
to knock bees from hyacinths

hydrangeas with nine heads
bloom with cockscomb breath—
winds, with frostbitten sabers
attempt to slay them again—

but no blade is ever drawn
without a dew by noon—
the sun, defender of flowers
lends his whips in March's duel!

whiskey blossoms

the Sweet Williams bloomed
after three days of rain—
all while i quarantined
to fill up on Jim Beam

where i grew overcast
of the sun for how swiftly
he abandoned, then reappeared
without consequence or advisory

for his unforecasted leave—
i wished my return would be
met with smiles and not questions
the perfume of me precipitates

echinacea echelon

blue balloon flowers
bolstered by
wrought iron bars—

climb for the
Johnny jump ups
inside suspended flower pots—

they both strive
to reach
the echinacea's echelon

where they can brush petals
with bergamots—
where the bees & butterflies are!

robin

i was met with a serenade
outside my window in May—
he threw no stone at my pane
just a glance or two between
his tune that carried harp strings
chords no guitar could creed—
yet still, my smile was enough applause
to keep him there all of spring

robin, why can't more men
be just as kind as you?
you have the wings to fly—
but stay, unlike they do

mantis

it would be more an honor
to have my shoulder be resting mound
for a haphazard headhuntress—

than it'd be to hold the hand
of a half-hearted man

pheromone

his body has ripe attar—
the extract of long labor—
the eau de pervasive
across his tendril covered chest!

he lifts his arms, inviting me
to frolic his musk meadows—
where i lick beads from filaments
like a nectar fiending bee!

dragonflies

the stained glass wings
of dragonflies can not
be shattered by boys
skipping rocks on the riverside

the only place they can go
to flick their wrist & compare lengths
outside overcast
of vitreous eyes

prince

i met a tiny prince
no bigger than my thumb—
he courted me with
an outstretched sweaty palm

then burrowed in my hand
as we crossed moated bog—
to introduce me to his kingdom
as a gentleman often does

then when it came time
for the two of us to depart—
he asked for no kiss
obliged by most
in modern tryst

his farewell was chivalrous
being but a leap—
then royal decree
to return tomorrow—
if i too shall please!

alpha

sadism does not make an alpha—
no man never misidentified
as less than because he aided
the pupa-wrestling butterfly

for i've seen too many men
attempt to crush out iridescence—
then recede & go ashen
for all the light they knocked out

but if he had the strength to lift it
closer to the sun—
to dry its damp watercolor
makes the heaviest weight
none

then if he waited by patient
for its wings to define—
to watch its first flight

makes him more a man
in my eyes

if we were bees
for Dawson

if we were bees
you'd always let
me decide on the pistil
we'd lay our heads

if we were birds
you'd always follow
when i flew from grass
to wire on impulse

if we were wolves
you'd always imprint
through terrain of tundra
if i waited at the end

if we were people
you'd always make sense
of my worries & burdens:
infinite as hives, brutal as pack

on butterfly wings

love finds you
on butterfly wings—
like wind finds the rain
so does the caterpillar a tree!

love hides, gone from the mind
like mayflies flee to find
lamps on below navy nights—
to feel the warmth of summertime

love can be a Monarch
an Emperor moth who decrees—
you care about yourself
the same way you do me

love can be out of sight
a presence better felt than seen—
like a butterfly, an angel can fly
without ever seeing its wings!

performative pollination

he sat atop a Sweet William
undeterred by pink—
then took his two front legs
to dismiss a dew
with vision linked

with scrutiny of his hive
who don't prefer, but submit—
to a single patch of clover
instead of flora they're prefixed—

which in colony's consciousness
is an unbefitting pollen
to the comb as a whole—
corrupting the larvae

who are preset to believe
that their floral inclination
should be in benefit
to the production of honey

capitalist comb

i blew from buttercup to clover
on breeze of an imperial order—
depleting each flower
i meet of nectar—
to keep comb from exposure

only permitted a hive
when dusted blond
& my share of honey due—

sleep, a far-off luxury
reduced to farmer—
not his fruit

with no wage or significance
paid to its laborers—
who works so their keeper
can sweeten his tea—
douse his bread

the beegeoisie

"All of this shows us that the bees are only obeying the laws which govern the economy of the hive, instead of a force outside of that economy, which compels them to make good a loss that man has brought about."
— *Gilbert M. Doolittle (beekeeper)*

there's a queen bee at the guillotine
in stocks of kadupul punishment—
her jury of human being,
bipartisan—in bereavement of honey

but bees are too few these days
to balance the scales of supply
& demand, so Insurrection
rears at one's Doolittle passion

hydrangeas & hierarchies shrivel—
the congress of comb elate
not at loss of their queen—but in man—
reckless in their uprising

when tomorrow comes, let them drink mead—
let them douse their honey on cake—
then when too late, let them notice too
how their modes of production—Annihilate

minnows

speak in maelstroms
a thousand times
their size

the fall of ancient Atlantis
the pitch of their
uprise

Charybdis fails in comparison—
she is only one
& civilization

need fleets
to bring forth
collapse—

no matter
how minute
the Insurgent

for the boys

for the boys who like flowers
with hair too short to braid
peonies into their
pompadoured manes—

for the lions who are careful
not to step on the daisies—
who don't need roar loudest
to remember they're kings!

for the boys who escape for hours
into the woods without company—
shake the spiderwebs from your hair
to avoid black widow dandruff

& remember, no wizard is ever shy
of bee or butterfly—
they'll stay for your nectar—
& you—the sunshine!

persimmons

persimmons fallen on the frost
saturate & make sanguine
the grounds of October's dawns

what creature of suburban orchard
would indulge in such sherbert
that splatter by plummet from
tree's fifteen foot purpose?

but who are we to judge Nature?
we too fend for fallen fruit

the wind secretes our speech
unbeknownst to the receive—

draws thistle to the skin's surface—
blooming blue, cause we humans
don't bruise so one-sided
as vermilion persimmons

Nature have ways
to camouflage pain
as something of symmetry,
where we humans fail syzygy

it reads not on us as rot
but the laying of sod—
carpentered, veneering
the cadaver beyond

that's why autumn is a lover
you cannot trust:
warm in the day,
frigid by dusk

at least winter is still—
stable enough for a promise
of spring on the horizon—
vases of Bonaparte roses in my dining

room, but for now
the house only smells
of the persimmons baking
in the late morning hour

no need for fertilizer
seasons
or harvest—

Nature unattended
is jarred marmalade

out of season

an "experienced" man
came down the trail
where Doe leave
her Fawn for bed

he with his rifle
came to seize a prize—
not to mount on his wall
but to measure his size

he wanted no antler
but indentions of velvet—
whose soft rub polished
his calloused weapon

with his slug fingers
he ran down my piebald—
darkening every white spot
like Communion suit to leather

with staggering knees
i attempted flee—
but my snare tightened
by sheer naiveté

Veal instead of Buck
i grew up in his cargo bed—
hung & then gutted
by a hunter, no man

candlelight

he burns like a candle
till snuffed by something you say—
then he flickers in & out
trying to reignite the flame

he smokes up your room
with rose & musk fumes
or whatever scent you choose—
name one so he won't assume

the worst when his wick
is left unattended—
so his worries won't leak wax
in solid streams onto your mahogany's
coffee-ringed covered sheen—
where he settles
deemed by you—
dirty

no trespassing

my brain is infested
with overactive arachnids—
who spin silk with adhesive
that grant no pollinator transit

without quandary to ascertain:
what is gossamer from axon,
balanced nectar from venom,
or passing thought from Sentence

poinsettias

Nature's final flower heeds
that we keep our fires burning—
when the clover loses its crimson
& the cardinals all toil for seed

this warmth is a privilege, the matches
that light our window candles
should not be snuffed just after Christmas—
the flowers won't blaze again till Spring

gold

has had prevalence
centuries in men's fashion:
on tomb of Tutankhamen—
laurels of Alexander the Great

my penchant for prosody
sows me no favor for Kingdom—
nor even trade of Plato's
that banishes lines of me

Priest, Politicians & Philosophers
have all told me the same—
that the Poet desecrates a pattern
already centuries plaid

no real man completely
forgoes his weight in gold—
for some lesser value that is
insubstantial to uphold

a foundation to raise
a family & a home—
but i've known these Stanzas
to hold more than Precious Stone!

house mouse

my existence has been a mouse—
the scurry gone unnoticed
at scrimmage of bowl & basket
after *Salute* of Sunday dinner

for their crumbs i've stayed in place—
inclement insulation between
spring-loaded steps & cheese—
the feast at human's deceive!

poet prodigy

i sample my memories
for a few saccharine snippets
to create deluges of lyric—
the fentanyl of the masses

my bandana is flood wall
that keeps hyacinthine locks
of syrupy mane from curling
into my eyes & thoughts

which attracts lines like flies
that have the buzz of bees—
& metaphors with no meaning
but real enough to bleed

i need be on these rhymes—
they're the only way bullets
don't take seed in my cortex—
all the rock n roll poets

sync with this same sentiment
of happiness contingent
on success counted sweetest
by those who ne'er receive

a kind word enough to say—
so write instead, in vain—
& taste, but never digest
the sickeningly sweetness of fame!

imposter syndrome

i envy the bird
closer to heaven—than i

the crackerjack-cardinal
who chirps
by empty feeder of mine

he sings of what divinity he's spoken—
& my own doubt made me agree
that his tune must be taken as twine
if its melody frayed my piety

that fluff of callous-carmine
can do what prayer promised
in half the time it takes
for my threadbared correspondence

to stitch with God through Gabriel—
in hopes to borrow an armor—
with saintly seamed feathers that plume
from the helmets of virtuosos!

nature's sermon

He drilled what rang like gospel
through the barren parished forest

He flailed no fire & brimstone—
just a few wood flurries for thermos

i felt contented by His sermon—
the pews all sinewy shafted

He asked no forced confession
or collection, beyond my attention

He preached, not of damnation
as He pulled grub from in Pine—

our Communion, when my eyes
met holy in His flight!

like a flower

like a flower
remain planted
don't let yourself be picked
you'll only wither in the embrace
of a cheap ceramic vase
keep yourself rooted
in the ground
don't get too involved
like a flower
available in spring
gone by fall

Jawn Van Jacobs is a poet and educator whose bastard bee takes a fresh look at masculinity through the lens of vulnerability and strength. By highlighting nature's overlooked creatures, Jawn brings a unique perspective to the queer experience. This collection is for all men, especially young queer individuals, showing how love and authenticity can lead to a richer life. With an MA in Writing Arts, Jawn teaches English Composition, fostering a supportive space for students to explore their identities. bastard bee blends vivid natural imagery with personal reflection, challenging traditional views on masculinity.